50 Thai Curry Simplified Recipes for Home

By: Kelly Johnson

Table of Contents

- Green Curry Chicken
- Red Curry Beef
- Massaman Curry with Tofu
- Panang Curry Pork
- Yellow Curry Shrimp
- Pineapple Curry Chicken
- Pumpkin Curry with Chickpeas
- Thai Basil Eggplant Curry
- Coconut Curry Vegetables
- Spicy Mango Curry Chicken
- Lemongrass Curry Tofu
- Thai Curry Fried Rice
- Curry Noodle Soup
- Thai Curry Potatoes
- Thai Curry Meatballs
- Thai Curry Quinoa
- Thai Curry Coconut Soup
- Thai Curry Stir-Fry
- Thai Curry Salmon
- Thai Curry Tempeh
- Thai Curry Stuffed Bell Peppers
- Thai Curry Hummus
- Thai Curry Chicken Wraps
- Thai Curry Lentil Soup
- Thai Curry Chickpea Salad
- Thai Curry Sweet Potatoes
- Thai Curry Pasta
- Thai Curry Cauliflower Steaks
- Thai Curry Stuffed Zucchini
- Thai Curry Avocado Toast
- Thai Curry Tofu Skewers
- Thai Curry Coconut Rice
- Thai Curry Cashew Dip
- Thai Curry Chickpea Stew
- Thai Curry Vegetable Spring Rolls

- Thai Curry Breakfast Hash
- Thai Curry Butternut Squash Soup
- Thai Curry Pita Pockets
- Thai Curry Rice Paper Rolls
- Thai Curry Veggie Burgers
- Thai Curry Couscous Salad
- Thai Curry Roasted Brussels Sprouts
- Thai Curry Zoodle Salad
- Thai Curry Corn Chowder
- Thai Curry Pizza
- Thai Curry Chickpea Curry
- Thai Curry Cucumber Salad
- Thai Curry Quinoa Salad
- Thai Curry Ratatouille
- Thai Curry Potato Salad

Green Curry Chicken

Ingredients:

- 1 lb (450g) boneless, skinless chicken breast, thinly sliced
- 1 can (13.5 oz) coconut milk
- 2-3 tablespoons green curry paste
- 1 cup mixed vegetables (such as bell peppers, bamboo shoots, and eggplant)
- 2 tablespoons fish sauce
- 1 tablespoon brown sugar
- 1 tablespoon vegetable oil
- 1 tablespoon minced garlic
- 1 tablespoon minced ginger
- 1 small onion, thinly sliced
- 1 cup fresh basil leaves
- Salt, to taste
- Cooked rice, for serving

Instructions:

Heat vegetable oil in a large skillet or wok over medium heat.
Add minced garlic, ginger, and sliced onion. Sauté until fragrant and onions are translucent, about 2-3 minutes.
Add green curry paste to the skillet and stir-fry for another minute.
Add sliced chicken breast to the skillet and cook until it starts to brown, about 5-6 minutes.
Pour in coconut milk, fish sauce, and brown sugar. Stir well to combine.
Add mixed vegetables to the skillet and simmer for 8-10 minutes or until chicken is cooked through and vegetables are tender.
Season with salt to taste.
Just before serving, stir in fresh basil leaves.
Serve hot over cooked rice. Enjoy your green curry chicken!

Red Curry Beef

Ingredients:

- 1 lb (450g) beef sirloin, thinly sliced
- 1 can (13.5 oz) coconut milk
- 2-3 tablespoons red curry paste
- 1 cup mixed vegetables (such as bell peppers, carrots, and snow peas)
- 2 tablespoons fish sauce
- 1 tablespoon brown sugar
- 1 tablespoon vegetable oil
- 1 tablespoon minced garlic
- 1 tablespoon minced ginger
- 1 small onion, thinly sliced
- 1 cup fresh basil leaves
- Salt, to taste
- Cooked rice, for serving

Instructions:

Heat vegetable oil in a large skillet or wok over medium heat.
Add minced garlic, ginger, and sliced onion. Sauté until fragrant and onions are translucent, about 2-3 minutes.
Add red curry paste to the skillet and stir-fry for another minute.
Add sliced beef to the skillet and cook until it starts to brown, about 3-4 minutes.
Pour in coconut milk, fish sauce, and brown sugar. Stir well to combine.
Add mixed vegetables to the skillet and simmer for 5-7 minutes or until beef is cooked to your liking and vegetables are tender.
Season with salt to taste.
Just before serving, stir in fresh basil leaves.
Serve hot over cooked rice. Enjoy your red curry beef!

Massaman Curry with Tofu

Ingredients:

- 1 block (14 oz) firm tofu, drained and cubed
- 1 can (13.5 oz) coconut milk
- 3 tablespoons Massaman curry paste
- 1 large potato, peeled and cubed
- 1 large carrot, peeled and sliced
- 1 onion, chopped
- 2 cloves garlic, minced
- 1 tablespoon minced ginger
- 2 tablespoons peanut oil or vegetable oil
- 2 tablespoons brown sugar
- 2 tablespoons soy sauce
- 1 tablespoon tamarind paste
- 1 cinnamon stick
- 3-4 cardamom pods
- 1 bay leaf
- 1/4 cup roasted peanuts, chopped (optional)
- Fresh cilantro, for garnish
- Cooked rice, for serving

Instructions:

Heat oil in a large skillet or pot over medium heat. Add minced garlic, ginger, and chopped onion. Sauté until fragrant and onions are softened, about 2-3 minutes. Add Massaman curry paste to the skillet and cook for another minute, stirring constantly.

Pour in coconut milk and stir well to combine with the curry paste.

Add cubed tofu, cubed potato, sliced carrot, cinnamon stick, cardamom pods, and bay leaf to the skillet. Stir to combine.

Bring the mixture to a simmer, then reduce the heat to low. Cover and cook for 15-20 minutes, or until the vegetables are tender.

Stir in brown sugar, soy sauce, and tamarind paste. Taste and adjust seasoning if needed.

If desired, add chopped roasted peanuts for extra crunch and flavor.

Serve hot over cooked rice, garnished with fresh cilantro. Enjoy your Massaman curry with tofu!

Panang Curry Pork
Ingredients:

- 1 lb (450g) pork tenderloin or pork loin, thinly sliced
- 1 can (13.5 oz) coconut milk
- 3 tablespoons Panang curry paste
- 1 red bell pepper, sliced
- 1 small onion, thinly sliced
- 2 cloves garlic, minced
- 1 tablespoon minced ginger
- 2 tablespoons peanut oil or vegetable oil
- 2 tablespoons fish sauce
- 1 tablespoon brown sugar
- 1 tablespoon lime juice
- 1/4 cup fresh basil leaves, torn
- 1/4 cup roasted peanuts, chopped (optional)
- Cooked rice, for serving

Instructions:

Heat oil in a large skillet or wok over medium heat. Add minced garlic, ginger, and sliced onion. Sauté until fragrant and onions are softened, about 2-3 minutes.
Add Panang curry paste to the skillet and cook for another minute, stirring constantly.
Pour in coconut milk and stir well to combine with the curry paste.
Add sliced pork to the skillet and cook until it starts to brown, about 3-4 minutes.
Add sliced red bell pepper to the skillet and stir to combine.
Season with fish sauce, brown sugar, and lime juice. Stir well.
Simmer for 10-12 minutes or until the pork is cooked through and the sauce has thickened slightly.
Just before serving, stir in torn basil leaves and chopped roasted peanuts for extra flavor and texture.
Serve hot over cooked rice. Enjoy your Panang curry pork!

Yellow Curry Shrimp

Ingredients:

- 1 lb (450g) shrimp, peeled and deveined
- 1 can (13.5 oz) coconut milk
- 3 tablespoons yellow curry paste
- 1 large potato, peeled and cubed
- 1 large carrot, peeled and sliced
- 1 onion, chopped
- 2 cloves garlic, minced
- 1 tablespoon minced ginger
- 2 tablespoons peanut oil or vegetable oil
- 2 tablespoons fish sauce
- 1 tablespoon brown sugar
- 1 tablespoon lime juice
- 1/4 cup fresh cilantro, chopped
- Cooked rice, for serving

Instructions:

Heat oil in a large skillet or wok over medium heat. Add minced garlic, ginger, and chopped onion. Sauté until fragrant and onions are softened, about 2-3 minutes.
Add yellow curry paste to the skillet and cook for another minute, stirring constantly.
Pour in coconut milk and stir well to combine with the curry paste.
Add cubed potato and sliced carrot to the skillet. Stir to combine.
Bring the mixture to a simmer, then reduce the heat to low. Cover and cook for 10-12 minutes, or until the vegetables are tender.
Add shrimp to the skillet and stir gently to combine.
Season with fish sauce, brown sugar, and lime juice. Stir well.
Simmer for another 3-4 minutes or until the shrimp is cooked through.
Just before serving, sprinkle chopped cilantro over the curry.
Serve hot over cooked rice. Enjoy your yellow curry shrimp!

Pineapple Curry Chicken

Ingredients:

- 1 lb (450g) boneless, skinless chicken breast, cut into bite-sized pieces
- 1 can (13.5 oz) coconut milk
- 3 tablespoons red curry paste
- 1 cup pineapple chunks (fresh or canned)
- 1 red bell pepper, sliced
- 1 small onion, thinly sliced
- 2 cloves garlic, minced
- 1 tablespoon minced ginger
- 2 tablespoons vegetable oil
- 2 tablespoons fish sauce
- 1 tablespoon brown sugar
- 1 tablespoon lime juice
- Fresh cilantro, chopped, for garnish
- Cooked rice, for serving

Instructions:

Heat vegetable oil in a large skillet or wok over medium heat. Add minced garlic, ginger, and sliced onion. Sauté until fragrant and onions are softened, about 2-3 minutes.
Add red curry paste to the skillet and cook for another minute, stirring constantly.
Pour in coconut milk and stir well to combine with the curry paste.
Add chicken pieces to the skillet and cook until they start to brown, about 5-6 minutes.
Add pineapple chunks and sliced red bell pepper to the skillet. Stir to combine.
Season with fish sauce, brown sugar, and lime juice. Stir well.
Simmer for 8-10 minutes or until the chicken is cooked through and the sauce has thickened slightly.
Taste and adjust seasoning if needed.
Serve hot over cooked rice, garnished with chopped cilantro. Enjoy your pineapple curry chicken!

Pumpkin Curry with Chickpeas

Ingredients:

- 2 cups pumpkin or butternut squash, peeled and diced
- 1 can (13.5 oz) coconut milk
- 1 can (15 oz) chickpeas, drained and rinsed
- 2 tablespoons red curry paste
- 1 small onion, chopped
- 2 cloves garlic, minced
- 1 tablespoon minced ginger
- 2 tablespoons vegetable oil
- 1 tablespoon soy sauce
- 1 tablespoon brown sugar
- 1 tablespoon lime juice
- 1 cup vegetable broth
- Salt and pepper, to taste
- Fresh cilantro, chopped, for garnish
- Cooked rice, for serving

Instructions:

Heat vegetable oil in a large skillet or pot over medium heat. Add minced garlic, ginger, and chopped onion. Sauté until fragrant and onions are softened, about 2-3 minutes.

Add red curry paste to the skillet and cook for another minute, stirring constantly.

Pour in coconut milk and vegetable broth. Stir well to combine with the curry paste.

Add diced pumpkin or butternut squash to the skillet. Stir to combine.

Bring the mixture to a simmer, then reduce the heat to low. Cover and cook for 15-20 minutes, or until the pumpkin is tender.

Add chickpeas to the skillet and stir gently to combine.

Season with soy sauce, brown sugar, lime juice, salt, and pepper. Stir well.

Simmer for another 5-7 minutes to allow the flavors to meld together.

Taste and adjust seasoning if needed.

Serve hot over cooked rice, garnished with chopped cilantro. Enjoy your pumpkin curry with chickpeas!

Thai Basil Eggplant Curry

Ingredients:

- 2 medium-sized eggplants, diced
- 1 can (13.5 oz) coconut milk
- 3 tablespoons red curry paste
- 1 red bell pepper, sliced
- 1 small onion, thinly sliced
- 2 cloves garlic, minced
- 1 tablespoon minced ginger
- 2 tablespoons vegetable oil
- 2 tablespoons soy sauce
- 1 tablespoon brown sugar
- 1 tablespoon lime juice
- 1 cup fresh basil leaves, torn
- Salt, to taste
- Cooked rice, for serving

Instructions:

Heat vegetable oil in a large skillet or wok over medium heat. Add minced garlic, ginger, and sliced onion. Sauté until fragrant and onions are softened, about 2-3 minutes.
Add red curry paste to the skillet and cook for another minute, stirring constantly.
Pour in coconut milk and stir well to combine with the curry paste.
Add diced eggplant and sliced red bell pepper to the skillet. Stir to combine.
Bring the mixture to a simmer, then reduce the heat to low. Cover and cook for 10-12 minutes, or until the eggplant is tender.
Season with soy sauce, brown sugar, and lime juice. Stir well.
Just before serving, stir in torn basil leaves.
Taste and adjust seasoning if needed, adding salt as desired.
Serve hot over cooked rice. Enjoy your Thai basil eggplant curry!

Coconut Curry Vegetables

Ingredients:

- 2 cups mixed vegetables (such as bell peppers, carrots, broccoli, cauliflower, and snap peas)
- 1 can (13.5 oz) coconut milk
- 2 tablespoons red curry paste
- 1 small onion, thinly sliced
- 2 cloves garlic, minced
- 1 tablespoon minced ginger
- 2 tablespoons vegetable oil
- 1 tablespoon soy sauce
- 1 tablespoon brown sugar
- 1 tablespoon lime juice
- Salt, to taste
- Fresh cilantro, chopped, for garnish
- Cooked rice, for serving

Instructions:

Heat vegetable oil in a large skillet or wok over medium heat. Add minced garlic, ginger, and sliced onion. Sauté until fragrant and onions are softened, about 2-3 minutes.

Add red curry paste to the skillet and cook for another minute, stirring constantly.

Pour in coconut milk and stir well to combine with the curry paste.

Add mixed vegetables to the skillet. Stir to combine.

Bring the mixture to a simmer, then reduce the heat to low. Cover and cook for 8-10 minutes, or until the vegetables are tender.

Season with soy sauce, brown sugar, and lime juice. Stir well.

Taste and adjust seasoning if needed, adding salt as desired.

Serve hot over cooked rice, garnished with chopped cilantro. Enjoy your coconut curry vegetables!

Spicy Mango Curry Chicken

Ingredients:

- 1 lb (450g) boneless, skinless chicken breast, cut into bite-sized pieces
- 1 ripe mango, peeled and diced
- 1 can (13.5 oz) coconut milk
- 3 tablespoons red curry paste
- 1 red bell pepper, sliced
- 1 small onion, thinly sliced
- 2 cloves garlic, minced
- 1 tablespoon minced ginger
- 2 tablespoons vegetable oil
- 1 tablespoon soy sauce
- 1 tablespoon brown sugar
- 1 tablespoon lime juice
- 1 teaspoon chili flakes (adjust to taste for desired spice level)
- Salt, to taste
- Fresh cilantro, chopped, for garnish
- Cooked rice, for serving

Instructions:

Heat vegetable oil in a large skillet or wok over medium heat. Add minced garlic, ginger, and sliced onion. Sauté until fragrant and onions are softened, about 2-3 minutes.

Add red curry paste to the skillet and cook for another minute, stirring constantly.

Pour in coconut milk and stir well to combine with the curry paste.

Add diced mango and sliced red bell pepper to the skillet. Stir to combine.

Bring the mixture to a simmer, then reduce the heat to low. Cover and cook for 10-12 minutes, or until the chicken is cooked through.

Season with soy sauce, brown sugar, lime juice, chili flakes, and salt. Stir well. Taste and adjust seasoning if needed.

Serve hot over cooked rice, garnished with chopped cilantro. Enjoy your spicy mango curry chicken!

Lemongrass Curry Tofu

Ingredients:

- 1 block (14 oz) firm tofu, drained and cubed
- 2 stalks lemongrass, outer leaves removed, finely chopped
- 1 can (13.5 oz) coconut milk
- 3 tablespoons green curry paste
- 1 red bell pepper, sliced
- 1 small onion, thinly sliced
- 2 cloves garlic, minced
- 1 tablespoon minced ginger
- 2 tablespoons vegetable oil
- 2 tablespoons soy sauce
- 1 tablespoon brown sugar
- 1 tablespoon lime juice
- Salt, to taste
- Fresh cilantro, chopped, for garnish
- Cooked rice, for serving

Instructions:

Heat vegetable oil in a large skillet or wok over medium heat. Add minced garlic, ginger, and sliced onion. Sauté until fragrant and onions are softened, about 2-3 minutes.
Add green curry paste and chopped lemongrass to the skillet. Cook for another minute, stirring constantly.
Pour in coconut milk and stir well to combine with the curry paste.
Add cubed tofu and sliced red bell pepper to the skillet. Stir to combine.
Bring the mixture to a simmer, then reduce the heat to low. Cover and cook for 10-12 minutes, or until the tofu is heated through.
Season with soy sauce, brown sugar, lime juice, and salt. Stir well.
Taste and adjust seasoning if needed.
Serve hot over cooked rice, garnished with chopped cilantro. Enjoy your lemongrass curry tofu!

Thai Curry Fried Rice

Ingredients:

- 3 cups cooked jasmine rice, preferably cooled
- 2 tablespoons vegetable oil
- 2 tablespoons Thai red curry paste
- 2 cloves garlic, minced
- 1 small onion, diced
- 1 red bell pepper, diced
- 1 cup mixed vegetables (such as peas, carrots, and corn)
- 2 eggs, beaten
- 2 tablespoons soy sauce
- 1 tablespoon fish sauce
- 1 tablespoon brown sugar
- 1/4 cup chopped green onions
- Fresh cilantro, chopped, for garnish
- Lime wedges, for serving

Instructions:

Heat vegetable oil in a large skillet or wok over medium-high heat.

Add minced garlic and Thai red curry paste to the skillet. Cook for 1 minute, stirring constantly.

Add diced onion and cook until softened, about 2-3 minutes.

Add diced red bell pepper and mixed vegetables. Stir-fry for another 2-3 minutes until vegetables are tender.

Push the vegetables to one side of the skillet and pour the beaten eggs onto the other side. Scramble the eggs until cooked through.

Add cooked jasmine rice to the skillet. Stir well to combine with the vegetables and eggs.

Pour soy sauce, fish sauce, and brown sugar over the rice mixture. Stir well to coat evenly.

Cook for another 3-4 minutes, stirring occasionally, until the rice is heated through and slightly crispy.

Taste and adjust seasoning if needed.

Sprinkle chopped green onions and cilantro over the fried rice.

Serve hot with lime wedges on the side. Enjoy your Thai curry fried rice!

Curry Noodle Soup

Ingredients:

- 8 oz (225g) rice noodles or egg noodles
- 1 tablespoon vegetable oil
- 2 tablespoons Thai red curry paste
- 2 cloves garlic, minced
- 1 tablespoon minced ginger
- 4 cups chicken or vegetable broth
- 1 can (13.5 oz) coconut milk
- 1 tablespoon soy sauce
- 1 tablespoon fish sauce
- 1 tablespoon brown sugar
- 2 cups mixed vegetables (such as bok choy, carrots, mushrooms, and bell peppers)
- 1 lb (450g) cooked chicken, sliced (optional)
- Fresh cilantro, chopped, for garnish
- Lime wedges, for serving

Instructions:

Cook the rice noodles or egg noodles according to the package instructions. Drain and set aside.

Heat vegetable oil in a large pot over medium heat. Add minced garlic, minced ginger, and Thai red curry paste. Cook for 1-2 minutes, stirring constantly.

Pour in chicken or vegetable broth and coconut milk. Stir well to combine.

Add soy sauce, fish sauce, and brown sugar. Stir well and bring the soup to a simmer.

Add mixed vegetables to the soup. Simmer for about 5-7 minutes, or until the vegetables are tender.

If using cooked chicken, add it to the soup and simmer until heated through.

Taste the soup and adjust seasoning if needed.

Divide the cooked noodles among serving bowls.

Ladle the hot soup over the noodles.

Garnish with chopped cilantro.

Serve hot with lime wedges on the side. Enjoy your curry noodle soup!

Thai Curry Potatoes

Ingredients:

- 4 medium potatoes, peeled and diced
- 1 can (13.5 oz) coconut milk
- 2 tablespoons Thai yellow curry paste
- 1 small onion, thinly sliced
- 2 cloves garlic, minced
- 1 tablespoon minced ginger
- 2 tablespoons vegetable oil
- 1 tablespoon soy sauce
- 1 tablespoon brown sugar
- 1 tablespoon lime juice
- Salt, to taste
- Fresh cilantro, chopped, for garnish
- Cooked rice, for serving

Instructions:

Heat vegetable oil in a large skillet or pot over medium heat. Add minced garlic, ginger, and sliced onion. Sauté until fragrant and onions are softened, about 2-3 minutes.

Add Thai yellow curry paste to the skillet and cook for another minute, stirring constantly.

Pour in coconut milk and stir well to combine with the curry paste.

Add diced potatoes to the skillet. Stir to combine.

Bring the mixture to a simmer, then reduce the heat to low. Cover and cook for 15-20 minutes, or until the potatoes are tender.

Season with soy sauce, brown sugar, and lime juice. Stir well.

Taste and adjust seasoning if needed, adding salt as desired.

Serve hot over cooked rice, garnished with chopped cilantro. Enjoy your Thai curry potatoes!

Thai Curry Meatballs

Ingredients:

For the meatballs:

- 1 lb (450g) ground beef or chicken
- 1/4 cup breadcrumbs
- 1 egg
- 2 cloves garlic, minced
- 1 tablespoon minced ginger
- 2 green onions, finely chopped
- 1 tablespoon soy sauce
- Salt and pepper, to taste

For the curry sauce:

- 1 can (13.5 oz) coconut milk
- 3 tablespoons red curry paste
- 1 tablespoon vegetable oil
- 1 small onion, finely chopped
- 2 cloves garlic, minced
- 1 tablespoon minced ginger
- 1 red bell pepper, thinly sliced
- 1 cup chicken or vegetable broth
- 2 tablespoons fish sauce
- 1 tablespoon brown sugar
- 1 tablespoon lime juice
- Fresh cilantro, chopped, for garnish
- Cooked rice or noodles, for serving

Instructions:

Preheat the oven to 400°F (200°C). Line a baking sheet with parchment paper.

In a large mixing bowl, combine ground meat, breadcrumbs, egg, minced garlic, minced ginger, chopped green onions, soy sauce, salt, and pepper. Mix until well combined.

Shape the mixture into meatballs, about 1 inch in diameter. Place them on the prepared baking sheet.

Bake the meatballs in the preheated oven for 15-20 minutes, or until cooked through and lightly browned.

While the meatballs are baking, prepare the curry sauce. Heat vegetable oil in a large skillet or pot over medium heat. Add chopped onion, minced garlic, and minced ginger. Sauté until fragrant and onions are softened, about 2-3 minutes.

Add red curry paste to the skillet and cook for another minute, stirring constantly.

Pour in coconut milk, chicken or vegetable broth, and sliced red bell pepper. Stir well to combine.

Add fish sauce, brown sugar, and lime juice to the skillet. Stir well and bring the mixture to a simmer.

Once the meatballs are cooked, add them to the skillet with the curry sauce. Gently stir to coat the meatballs in the sauce.

Simmer for another 5-7 minutes to allow the flavors to meld together and the sauce to thicken slightly.

Taste and adjust seasoning if needed.

Serve the Thai curry meatballs hot over cooked rice or noodles, garnished with chopped cilantro. Enjoy!

Thai Curry Quinoa

Ingredients:

- 1 cup quinoa, rinsed
- 1 can (13.5 oz) coconut milk
- 3 tablespoons red curry paste
- 1 small onion, diced
- 2 cloves garlic, minced
- 1 tablespoon minced ginger
- 1 red bell pepper, diced
- 1 cup mixed vegetables (such as carrots, peas, and corn)
- 1 tablespoon vegetable oil
- 2 tablespoons soy sauce
- 1 tablespoon brown sugar
- 1 tablespoon lime juice
- Salt, to taste
- Fresh cilantro, chopped, for garnish

Instructions:

In a medium saucepan, combine quinoa with 2 cups of water. Bring to a boil, then reduce the heat to low, cover, and simmer for 15-20 minutes, or until the quinoa is cooked and the water is absorbed. Remove from heat and let it sit, covered, for 5 minutes. Fluff with a fork and set aside.

In a large skillet or wok, heat vegetable oil over medium heat. Add diced onion, minced garlic, and minced ginger. Sauté until fragrant and onions are softened, about 2-3 minutes.

Add red curry paste to the skillet and cook for another minute, stirring constantly. Pour in coconut milk and stir well to combine with the curry paste.

Add diced red bell pepper and mixed vegetables to the skillet. Stir to combine. Bring the mixture to a simmer, then reduce the heat to low. Cover and cook for 8-10 minutes, or until the vegetables are tender.

Add cooked quinoa to the skillet and stir well to combine with the curry mixture. Season with soy sauce, brown sugar, lime juice, and salt. Stir well.

Taste and adjust seasoning if needed.

Serve hot, garnished with chopped cilantro. Enjoy your Thai curry quinoa!

Thai Curry Coconut Soup

Ingredients:

- 1 can (13.5 oz) coconut milk
- 3 cups vegetable or chicken broth
- 2 tablespoons Thai red curry paste
- 1 tablespoon vegetable oil
- 1 small onion, finely chopped
- 2 cloves garlic, minced
- 1 tablespoon minced ginger
- 1 red bell pepper, thinly sliced
- 1 cup mixed vegetables (such as carrots, mushrooms, and snow peas)
- 1 can (14 oz) bamboo shoots, drained and sliced
- 1 cup firm tofu, cubed
- 2 tablespoons soy sauce
- 1 tablespoon brown sugar
- 1 tablespoon lime juice
- Salt, to taste
- Fresh cilantro, chopped, for garnish
- Cooked rice or rice noodles, for serving

Instructions:

Heat vegetable oil in a large pot over medium heat. Add chopped onion, minced garlic, and minced ginger. Sauté until fragrant and onions are softened, about 2-3 minutes.

Add Thai red curry paste to the pot and cook for another minute, stirring constantly.

Pour in coconut milk and vegetable or chicken broth. Stir well to combine.

Add thinly sliced red bell pepper, mixed vegetables, bamboo shoots, and cubed tofu to the pot. Stir to combine.

Bring the soup to a simmer and cook for about 10-15 minutes, or until the vegetables are tender and the tofu is heated through.

Season with soy sauce, brown sugar, lime juice, and salt. Stir well.

Taste and adjust seasoning if needed.

Serve hot, garnished with chopped cilantro.

If desired, serve the soup over cooked rice or rice noodles. Enjoy your Thai curry coconut soup!

Thai Curry Stir-Fry

Ingredients:

- 1 lb (450g) protein of choice (chicken breast, shrimp, tofu, beef), thinly sliced or cubed
- 2 tablespoons Thai curry paste (red, green, or yellow)
- 2 tablespoons vegetable oil
- 1 onion, thinly sliced
- 2 cloves garlic, minced
- 1 tablespoon minced ginger
- 2 bell peppers, thinly sliced
- 2 cups mixed vegetables (such as broccoli, snap peas, carrots)
- 1 can (13.5 oz) coconut milk
- 2 tablespoons soy sauce
- 1 tablespoon fish sauce
- 1 tablespoon brown sugar
- 1 tablespoon lime juice
- Fresh basil leaves or cilantro, chopped, for garnish
- Cooked rice or noodles, for serving

Instructions:

Heat vegetable oil in a large skillet or wok over medium-high heat.
Add minced garlic, minced ginger, and Thai curry paste to the skillet. Cook for 1-2 minutes, stirring constantly.
Add thinly sliced protein (chicken, shrimp, tofu, beef) to the skillet. Cook until the protein is browned and cooked through.
Add thinly sliced onion and bell peppers to the skillet. Stir-fry for another 2-3 minutes until they start to soften.
Add mixed vegetables to the skillet. Stir-fry for an additional 2-3 minutes until the vegetables are tender-crisp.
Pour in coconut milk, soy sauce, fish sauce, brown sugar, and lime juice. Stir well to combine.
Continue cooking for another 2-3 minutes until the sauce thickens slightly and coats the ingredients.
Taste and adjust seasoning if needed.
Serve hot over cooked rice or noodles.
Garnish with chopped fresh basil leaves or cilantro.
Enjoy your Thai curry stir-fry!

Thai Curry Salmon

Ingredients:

- 4 salmon fillets (about 6 oz each)
- 2 tablespoons Thai red curry paste
- 1 can (13.5 oz) coconut milk
- 2 tablespoons soy sauce
- 1 tablespoon fish sauce
- 1 tablespoon brown sugar
- 1 tablespoon lime juice
- 2 cloves garlic, minced
- 1 tablespoon minced ginger
- 1 tablespoon vegetable oil
- Fresh cilantro, chopped, for garnish
- Lime wedges, for serving
- Cooked rice or noodles, for serving

Instructions:

In a small bowl, mix together Thai red curry paste, minced garlic, minced ginger, soy sauce, fish sauce, brown sugar, and lime juice to make the marinade.

Place the salmon fillets in a shallow dish and pour the marinade over them.

Ensure the fillets are well coated. Let them marinate for at least 30 minutes in the refrigerator.

Heat vegetable oil in a large skillet over medium-high heat.

Remove the salmon fillets from the marinade and shake off any excess marinade.

Place the salmon fillets in the skillet, skin-side down. Cook for 3-4 minutes, or until the skin is crispy and browned.

Flip the salmon fillets and cook for another 2-3 minutes, or until the salmon is cooked through and flakes easily with a fork.

While the salmon is cooking, pour the remaining marinade into the skillet.

Add coconut milk to the skillet and stir well to combine with the marinade.

Bring the sauce to a simmer and cook for 2-3 minutes until slightly thickened.

Serve the salmon hot over cooked rice or noodles.

Spoon the curry sauce over the salmon fillets.

Garnish with chopped fresh cilantro and serve with lime wedges on the side.

Enjoy your Thai curry salmon!

Thai Curry Tempeh

Ingredients:

- 8 oz (225g) tempeh, sliced into strips or cubes
- 2 tablespoons Thai red curry paste
- 1 can (13.5 oz) coconut milk
- 1 tablespoon soy sauce
- 1 tablespoon fish sauce (optional for non-vegetarian)
- 1 tablespoon brown sugar
- 1 tablespoon lime juice
- 2 cloves garlic, minced
- 1 tablespoon minced ginger
- 1 tablespoon vegetable oil
- 1 red bell pepper, thinly sliced
- 1 small onion, thinly sliced
- 2 cups mixed vegetables (such as broccoli, snap peas, and carrots)
- Fresh cilantro, chopped, for garnish
- Cooked rice or noodles, for serving

Instructions:

Heat vegetable oil in a large skillet or wok over medium heat.
Add minced garlic, minced ginger, and Thai red curry paste to the skillet. Cook for 1-2 minutes, stirring constantly.
Add tempeh to the skillet and cook until lightly browned, about 4-5 minutes.
Add thinly sliced red bell pepper, thinly sliced onion, and mixed vegetables to the skillet. Stir-fry for another 2-3 minutes until the vegetables are tender-crisp.
Pour in coconut milk, soy sauce, fish sauce (if using), brown sugar, and lime juice. Stir well to combine.
Bring the mixture to a simmer and cook for about 5-7 minutes until the sauce thickens slightly and coats the tempeh and vegetables.
Taste and adjust seasoning if needed.
Serve hot over cooked rice or noodles.
Garnish with chopped fresh cilantro.
Enjoy your Thai curry tempeh!

Thai Curry Stuffed Bell Peppers

Ingredients:

- 4 large bell peppers, any color
- 1 cup cooked rice (white or brown)
- 1 can (13.5 oz) coconut milk
- 2 tablespoons Thai red curry paste
- 1 tablespoon vegetable oil
- 1 small onion, finely chopped
- 2 cloves garlic, minced
- 1 tablespoon minced ginger
- 1 cup mixed vegetables (such as carrots, peas, and corn)
- 8 oz (225g) firm tofu, diced
- 1 tablespoon soy sauce
- 1 tablespoon fish sauce (optional)
- 1 tablespoon brown sugar
- 1 tablespoon lime juice
- Salt, to taste
- Fresh cilantro, chopped, for garnish

Instructions:

Preheat the oven to 375°F (190°C).

Cut the tops off the bell peppers and remove the seeds and membranes. Place the hollowed-out bell peppers in a baking dish and set aside.

In a large skillet, heat vegetable oil over medium heat. Add chopped onion, minced garlic, and minced ginger. Sauté until fragrant and onions are softened, about 2-3 minutes.

Add Thai red curry paste to the skillet and cook for another minute, stirring constantly.

Pour in coconut milk and stir well to combine with the curry paste.

Add cooked rice, mixed vegetables, and diced tofu to the skillet. Stir to combine. Season with soy sauce, fish sauce (if using), brown sugar, lime juice, and salt. Stir well.

Simmer the mixture for 5-7 minutes, stirring occasionally, until heated through and the flavors meld together.

Spoon the curry mixture into the hollowed-out bell peppers until they are filled to the top.

Cover the baking dish with aluminum foil and bake in the preheated oven for 25-30 minutes, or until the bell peppers are tender.

Remove the foil and bake for an additional 5-10 minutes if you prefer the bell peppers to be slightly charred.

Serve hot, garnished with chopped fresh cilantro.

Enjoy your Thai curry stuffed bell peppers!

Thai Curry Hummus

Ingredients:

- 1 can (15 oz) chickpeas, drained and rinsed
- 2 tablespoons tahini
- 2 tablespoons olive oil
- 2 cloves garlic, minced
- 2 tablespoons Thai red curry paste
- 2 tablespoons fresh lime juice
- 1 teaspoon soy sauce or tamari
- 1/4 cup coconut milk
- Salt, to taste
- Optional garnishes: chopped cilantro, chopped peanuts, red pepper flakes

Instructions:

In a food processor, combine the chickpeas, tahini, olive oil, garlic, red curry paste, lime juice, soy sauce, and coconut milk.
Blend until smooth, scraping down the sides of the bowl as needed to ensure all ingredients are incorporated.
Taste the hummus and adjust seasoning with salt as needed.
If the hummus is too thick, you can add more coconut milk or water, a tablespoon at a time, until you reach your desired consistency.
Transfer the hummus to a serving bowl and garnish with chopped cilantro, chopped peanuts, and red pepper flakes if desired.
Serve with pita bread, crackers, vegetable sticks, or use as a spread in sandwiches or wraps.

Enjoy the unique flavors of Thai curry infused into this creamy and delicious hummus!

Thai Curry Chicken Wraps

Ingredients:

- 1 lb boneless, skinless chicken breasts, thinly sliced
- 2 tablespoons Thai red curry paste
- 1 tablespoon soy sauce
- 1 tablespoon fish sauce
- 1 tablespoon brown sugar
- 1 tablespoon lime juice
- 1 tablespoon vegetable oil
- 1 red bell pepper, thinly sliced
- 1 yellow bell pepper, thinly sliced
- 1 small red onion, thinly sliced
- 1 cup shredded cabbage or coleslaw mix
- Fresh cilantro leaves, for garnish
- 4 large flour tortillas or wraps
- Optional: sliced cucumber, shredded carrots, sliced avocado

Instructions:

In a small bowl, whisk together the Thai red curry paste, soy sauce, fish sauce, brown sugar, and lime juice to make the marinade.
Place the thinly sliced chicken breasts in a shallow dish or resealable plastic bag. Pour the marinade over the chicken, ensuring it's well coated. Marinate in the refrigerator for at least 30 minutes, or preferably up to 4 hours.
Heat the vegetable oil in a large skillet over medium-high heat. Add the marinated chicken slices and cook until browned and cooked through, about 5-6 minutes per side. Remove the chicken from the skillet and set aside.
In the same skillet, add the sliced bell peppers and red onion. Cook, stirring occasionally, until the vegetables are tender-crisp, about 3-4 minutes.
Warm the flour tortillas or wraps according to package instructions.
To assemble the wraps, place a spoonful of shredded cabbage or coleslaw mix down the center of each tortilla. Top with cooked chicken slices, sautéed bell peppers and onions, and any optional toppings you desire.
Garnish with fresh cilantro leaves.
Fold in the sides of the tortilla and roll up tightly to enclose the filling.
Serve the Thai Curry Chicken Wraps immediately, either whole or sliced in half, with extra lime wedges on the side for squeezing.

Enjoy these flavorful and satisfying wraps, perfect for a quick lunch or dinner!

Thai Curry Lentil Soup

Ingredients:

- 1 cup dried red lentils, rinsed and drained
- 1 tablespoon olive oil or coconut oil
- 1 onion, diced
- 3 cloves garlic, minced
- 1 tablespoon fresh ginger, minced
- 2 tablespoons Thai red curry paste
- 1 teaspoon ground turmeric
- 1 teaspoon ground cumin
- 4 cups vegetable broth or chicken broth
- 1 can (14 oz) coconut milk
- 1 tablespoon soy sauce or tamari
- 1 tablespoon brown sugar or maple syrup
- Juice of 1 lime
- Salt and pepper, to taste
- Optional garnishes: chopped cilantro, sliced green onions, lime wedges, red pepper flakes

Instructions:

Heat the olive oil or coconut oil in a large pot over medium heat. Add the diced onion and cook until softened, about 5 minutes.

Add the minced garlic and ginger to the pot and cook for an additional 1-2 minutes, until fragrant.

Stir in the Thai red curry paste, ground turmeric, and ground cumin, and cook for another minute to toast the spices.

Add the rinsed red lentils to the pot, followed by the vegetable broth or chicken broth. Bring the mixture to a boil, then reduce the heat to low and let it simmer, partially covered, for about 20-25 minutes, or until the lentils are tender.

Stir in the coconut milk, soy sauce or tamari, brown sugar or maple syrup, and lime juice. Season with salt and pepper to taste.

Continue to simmer the soup for another 5-10 minutes to allow the flavors to meld together.

If desired, use an immersion blender to partially blend the soup to achieve a creamier texture while still leaving some lentils whole.

Taste and adjust seasoning as needed.

Serve the Thai Curry Lentil Soup hot, garnished with chopped cilantro, sliced green onions, a wedge of lime, and a sprinkle of red pepper flakes for added heat.

Enjoy this aromatic and hearty soup as a comforting meal on a chilly day!

Thai Curry Chickpea Salad

Ingredients:

- 2 cans (15 oz each) chickpeas, drained and rinsed
- 1 red bell pepper, diced
- 1 cucumber, diced
- 1/2 red onion, finely chopped
- 1/4 cup chopped fresh cilantro
- 1/4 cup chopped fresh mint leaves
- 1/4 cup chopped roasted peanuts or cashews
- 1/4 cup shredded coconut (optional)
- Juice of 2 limes
- 2 tablespoons olive oil
- 2 tablespoons Thai red curry paste
- 1 tablespoon honey or maple syrup
- Salt and pepper, to taste
- Optional garnish: lime wedges, additional chopped cilantro or mint

Instructions:

In a large mixing bowl, combine the drained and rinsed chickpeas, diced red bell pepper, diced cucumber, finely chopped red onion, chopped cilantro, chopped mint leaves, chopped roasted peanuts or cashews, and shredded coconut (if using).

In a small bowl, whisk together the lime juice, olive oil, Thai red curry paste, and honey or maple syrup until well combined.

Pour the dressing over the chickpea salad and toss gently to coat all the ingredients evenly.

Season the salad with salt and pepper to taste.

Allow the salad to marinate in the refrigerator for at least 30 minutes before serving to allow the flavors to meld together.

Before serving, taste and adjust the seasoning if needed.

Serve the Thai Curry Chickpea Salad chilled, garnished with lime wedges and additional chopped cilantro or mint if desired.

Enjoy this vibrant and flavorful salad as a refreshing side dish or a light and healthy lunch option!

Thai Curry Sweet Potatoes

Ingredients:

- 2 large sweet potatoes, peeled and diced into bite-sized cubes
- 2 tablespoons olive oil
- 2 tablespoons Thai red curry paste
- 1 tablespoon soy sauce or tamari
- 1 tablespoon honey or maple syrup
- 1 tablespoon lime juice
- 2 cloves garlic, minced
- 1 teaspoon grated fresh ginger
- Salt and pepper, to taste
- Optional garnish: chopped fresh cilantro, sliced green onions, toasted sesame seeds

Instructions:

Preheat your oven to 400°F (200°C).

In a large bowl, combine the diced sweet potatoes with olive oil, Thai red curry paste, soy sauce or tamari, honey or maple syrup, lime juice, minced garlic, and grated ginger. Toss until the sweet potatoes are evenly coated with the marinade.

Spread the coated sweet potatoes in a single layer on a baking sheet lined with parchment paper or aluminum foil.

Season the sweet potatoes with salt and pepper to taste.

Roast the sweet potatoes in the preheated oven for 25-30 minutes, or until they are tender and lightly browned, stirring halfway through the cooking time for even browning.

Once the sweet potatoes are cooked through, remove them from the oven and transfer them to a serving dish.

Garnish the Thai Curry Sweet Potatoes with chopped fresh cilantro, sliced green onions, and toasted sesame seeds if desired.

Serve hot as a flavorful side dish or incorporate them into Buddha bowls, salads, or wraps.

Enjoy these Thai Curry Sweet Potatoes as a delicious and nutritious addition to your meals!

Thai Curry Pasta

Ingredients:

- 8 oz (about 225g) pasta (linguine, spaghetti, or any preferred type)
- 2 tablespoons olive oil
- 1 onion, finely chopped
- 2 cloves garlic, minced
- 2 tablespoons Thai red curry paste
- 1 can (14 oz) coconut milk
- 1 red bell pepper, thinly sliced
- 1 green bell pepper, thinly sliced
- 1 carrot, julienned or thinly sliced
- 1 zucchini, thinly sliced
- 1 cup broccoli florets
- 1 tablespoon soy sauce or tamari
- 1 tablespoon brown sugar or coconut sugar
- Juice of 1 lime
- Salt and pepper, to taste
- Fresh cilantro leaves, for garnish
- Crushed peanuts or cashews, for garnish (optional)

Instructions:

Cook the pasta according to package instructions until al dente. Drain and set aside.

In a large skillet or wok, heat the olive oil over medium heat. Add the chopped onion and cook until translucent, about 3-4 minutes.

Add the minced garlic and Thai red curry paste to the skillet. Cook for an additional 1-2 minutes, stirring constantly, until fragrant.

Pour in the coconut milk and stir until the curry paste is fully incorporated.

Add the sliced bell peppers, julienned carrot, sliced zucchini, and broccoli florets to the skillet. Stir to coat the vegetables with the curry sauce.

Cook the vegetables for about 5-7 minutes, or until they are tender-crisp.

Stir in the soy sauce or tamari, brown sugar or coconut sugar, and lime juice. Season with salt and pepper to taste.

Add the cooked pasta to the skillet and toss until it is well coated with the Thai curry sauce and vegetables.

Cook for an additional 2-3 minutes, allowing the flavors to meld together.

Remove the skillet from heat and garnish the Thai Curry Pasta with fresh cilantro leaves and crushed peanuts or cashews (if using).
Serve hot and enjoy your delicious Thai Curry Pasta!

This dish is both flavorful and versatile, making it a perfect meal for lunch or dinner. Feel free to adjust the spice level and add your favorite vegetables or protein for a customized twist.

Thai Curry Cauliflower Steaks

Ingredients:

- 1 large head of cauliflower
- 3 tablespoons olive oil
- 2 tablespoons Thai red curry paste
- 2 tablespoons coconut milk
- 1 tablespoon soy sauce or tamari
- 1 tablespoon lime juice
- 2 cloves garlic, minced
- 1 teaspoon grated fresh ginger
- Salt and pepper, to taste
- Fresh cilantro leaves, for garnish
- Lime wedges, for serving

Instructions:

Preheat your oven to 425°F (220°C). Line a baking sheet with parchment paper or lightly grease it with olive oil.

Trim the leaves and stem of the cauliflower, leaving the core intact. Slice the cauliflower into 1-inch thick "steaks" by cutting vertically through the center of the cauliflower head. You should get 2-3 large steaks, depending on the size of your cauliflower.

In a small bowl, whisk together the olive oil, Thai red curry paste, coconut milk, soy sauce or tamari, lime juice, minced garlic, and grated ginger to make the marinade.

Place the cauliflower steaks on the prepared baking sheet. Brush both sides of the cauliflower steaks generously with the marinade, reserving some marinade for later use.

Season the cauliflower steaks with salt and pepper to taste.

Roast the cauliflower steaks in the preheated oven for 20-25 minutes, or until they are tender and golden brown, flipping halfway through the cooking time and brushing with additional marinade.

Once the cauliflower steaks are cooked through, remove them from the oven and transfer them to a serving platter.

Drizzle any remaining marinade over the cauliflower steaks and garnish with fresh cilantro leaves.

Serve the Thai Curry Cauliflower Steaks hot, accompanied by lime wedges for squeezing.

Enjoy these flavorful and satisfying cauliflower steaks as a delicious vegetarian main course or as a flavorful side dish!

Thai Curry Stuffed Zucchini

Ingredients:

- 4 medium zucchini
- 1 tablespoon olive oil
- 1 onion, finely chopped
- 2 cloves garlic, minced
- 1 tablespoon Thai red curry paste
- 1 can (14 oz) coconut milk
- 1 red bell pepper, diced
- 1 carrot, grated
- 1 cup cooked quinoa or rice
- Salt and pepper, to taste
- Fresh cilantro leaves, for garnish
- Lime wedges, for serving

Instructions:

Preheat your oven to 375°F (190°C).
Cut the zucchini in half lengthwise and scoop out the seeds and flesh, leaving about 1/4 inch thick shell. Reserve the scooped-out flesh for later use. Place the hollowed-out zucchini halves on a baking sheet lined with parchment paper.
Heat olive oil in a large skillet over medium heat. Add chopped onion and minced garlic, and cook until softened, about 3-4 minutes.
Add Thai red curry paste to the skillet and cook for another minute, stirring constantly.
Pour in the coconut milk and stir until well combined with the curry paste.
Add diced red bell pepper, grated carrot, and the reserved zucchini flesh to the skillet. Cook for about 5 minutes, or until the vegetables are tender.
Stir in cooked quinoa or rice into the skillet, and season with salt and pepper to taste. Cook for another 2-3 minutes to heat through and allow flavors to meld.
Spoon the quinoa or rice mixture into the hollowed-out zucchini halves, pressing gently to pack the filling.
Bake the stuffed zucchini in the preheated oven for 20-25 minutes, or until the zucchini is tender and the filling is heated through.
Remove the stuffed zucchini from the oven and garnish with fresh cilantro leaves.
Serve hot, accompanied by lime wedges for squeezing.

Enjoy these Thai Curry Stuffed Zucchini as a delicious and nutritious vegetarian main course or as a flavorful side dish!

Thai Curry Avocado Toast

Ingredients:

- 2 slices of your favorite bread (such as whole grain or sourdough)
- 1 ripe avocado
- 1 tablespoon Thai red curry paste
- 1 tablespoon lime juice
- Salt and pepper, to taste
- Optional toppings: sliced cherry tomatoes, sliced cucumber, chopped cilantro, toasted sesame seeds, crushed red pepper flakes

Instructions:

Toast the slices of bread to your desired level of crispiness.
While the bread is toasting, prepare the avocado spread. Scoop the flesh of the ripe avocado into a bowl and mash it with a fork until smooth.
Add Thai red curry paste and lime juice to the mashed avocado. Stir until well combined and smooth. Season with salt and pepper to taste.
Once the bread is toasted, spread the Thai curry avocado mixture evenly onto each slice.
Top the avocado toast with your favorite toppings such as sliced cherry tomatoes, sliced cucumber, chopped cilantro, toasted sesame seeds, or crushed red pepper flakes.
Serve immediately and enjoy your Thai Curry Avocado Toast as a delicious and satisfying breakfast, brunch, or snack option!

This flavorful twist on avocado toast is sure to delight your taste buds with its creamy texture and aromatic Thai curry flavor. Feel free to customize the toppings according to your preferences and enjoy this tasty dish any time of day!

Thai Curry Tofu Skewers

Ingredients:

- 1 block (14-16 oz) extra firm tofu, pressed and drained
- 2 tablespoons Thai red curry paste
- 2 tablespoons coconut milk
- 1 tablespoon soy sauce or tamari
- 1 tablespoon lime juice
- 2 cloves garlic, minced
- 1 teaspoon grated fresh ginger
- 1 tablespoon olive oil or vegetable oil
- Salt and pepper, to taste
- Bamboo skewers, soaked in water for 30 minutes
- Optional garnishes: chopped cilantro, sliced green onions, lime wedges

Instructions:

Preheat your grill to medium-high heat or preheat your oven to 400°F (200°C).
Cut the pressed and drained tofu block into cubes, about 1 inch in size.
In a small bowl, whisk together the Thai red curry paste, coconut milk, soy sauce or tamari, lime juice, minced garlic, and grated ginger to make the marinade.
Place the tofu cubes in a shallow dish or resealable plastic bag. Pour the marinade over the tofu and toss gently to coat all the cubes evenly. Let the tofu marinate for at least 30 minutes, or preferably up to 2 hours, in the refrigerator.
If grilling, thread the marinated tofu cubes onto the soaked bamboo skewers, leaving a little space between each cube.
If baking, place the marinated tofu cubes on a baking sheet lined with parchment paper or aluminum foil.
Brush the tofu skewers or cubes with olive oil or vegetable oil to prevent sticking.
Grill the tofu skewers over medium-high heat for 10-12 minutes, turning occasionally, until the tofu is lightly charred and heated through.
If baking, place the baking sheet in the preheated oven and bake for 20-25 minutes, or until the tofu is golden brown and crispy around the edges.
Once the tofu is cooked, remove it from the grill or oven and let it cool for a few minutes.
Serve the Thai Curry Tofu Skewers hot, garnished with chopped cilantro, sliced green onions, and lime wedges if desired.

Enjoy these flavorful and protein-rich Thai Curry Tofu Skewers as a delicious appetizer, main course, or side dish!

Thai Curry Coconut Rice

Ingredients:

- 1 cup jasmine rice (or any long-grain rice)
- 1 cup coconut milk
- 1 cup water
- 1 tablespoon Thai red curry paste
- 1 tablespoon vegetable oil
- 1 teaspoon sugar (optional)
- 1/2 teaspoon salt, or to taste
- 1 tablespoon chopped fresh cilantro (optional, for garnish)
- Lime wedges, for serving (optional)

Instructions:

Rinse the rice in cold water until the water runs clear. This helps remove excess starch and prevents the rice from becoming too sticky.

In a medium saucepan, heat the vegetable oil over medium heat. Add the Thai red curry paste and cook for 1-2 minutes, stirring constantly, until fragrant.

Pour in the coconut milk and water, and stir until the curry paste is fully dissolved and well combined with the liquid.

Add the rinsed rice to the saucepan and stir to combine. Bring the mixture to a gentle boil.

Once boiling, reduce the heat to low, cover the saucepan with a lid, and simmer for about 15-20 minutes, or until the rice is tender and the liquid is absorbed. Avoid stirring the rice during cooking to prevent it from becoming mushy.

Once the rice is cooked, remove the saucepan from the heat and let it sit, covered, for 5 minutes to allow the rice to steam.

Fluff the rice with a fork to separate the grains. Taste and adjust the seasoning with salt and sugar if desired.

Transfer the Thai Curry Coconut Rice to a serving dish and garnish with chopped fresh cilantro, if using.

Serve the rice hot, accompanied by lime wedges for squeezing if desired.

Enjoy this aromatic and creamy Thai Curry Coconut Rice as a delicious side dish to complement your favorite Thai-inspired meals!

Thai Curry Cashew Dip

Ingredients:

- 1 cup raw cashews, soaked in water for at least 4 hours or overnight
- 2 tablespoons Thai red curry paste
- 1 tablespoon lime juice
- 2 cloves garlic, minced
- 2 tablespoons coconut milk
- 1 tablespoon soy sauce or tamari
- 1 tablespoon maple syrup or honey
- Salt, to taste
- Water, as needed for thinning consistency
- Optional garnishes: chopped cilantro, chopped green onions, crushed red pepper flakes

Instructions:

After soaking the cashews, drain and rinse them thoroughly.
In a food processor or high-speed blender, combine the soaked cashews, Thai red curry paste, lime juice, minced garlic, coconut milk, soy sauce or tamari, and maple syrup or honey.
Blend the ingredients until smooth and creamy, scraping down the sides of the processor or blender as needed to ensure everything is well combined.
If the dip is too thick, you can add water, a tablespoon at a time, until you reach your desired consistency.
Taste the dip and adjust the seasoning with salt if needed.
Transfer the Thai Curry Cashew Dip to a serving bowl.
Garnish with chopped cilantro, chopped green onions, and crushed red pepper flakes if desired.
Serve the dip with sliced vegetables, crackers, or use as a spread in sandwiches or wraps.

Enjoy this flavorful and creamy Thai Curry Cashew Dip as a delicious appetizer or snack!

Thai Curry Chickpea Stew

Ingredients:

- 2 tablespoons vegetable oil
- 1 onion, finely chopped
- 3 cloves garlic, minced
- 1 tablespoon grated ginger
- 2 tablespoons Thai red curry paste
- 1 can (14 oz) coconut milk
- 1 can (15 oz) chickpeas, drained and rinsed
- 2 cups vegetable broth
- 1 red bell pepper, diced
- 1 carrot, diced
- 1 zucchini, diced
- 1 cup chopped spinach or kale
- 1 tablespoon soy sauce or tamari
- 1 tablespoon brown sugar or maple syrup
- Juice of 1 lime
- Salt and pepper, to taste
- Cooked rice or quinoa, for serving
- Fresh cilantro, chopped, for garnish

Instructions:

In a large pot or Dutch oven, heat the vegetable oil over medium heat. Add the chopped onion and cook until softened, about 5 minutes.
Add the minced garlic and grated ginger to the pot and cook for an additional 1-2 minutes, until fragrant.
Stir in the Thai red curry paste and cook for another minute to toast the spices.
Pour in the coconut milk and vegetable broth, stirring to combine.
Add the drained and rinsed chickpeas, diced red bell pepper, diced carrot, and diced zucchini to the pot. Stir to combine.
Bring the stew to a simmer and let it cook for about 15-20 minutes, until the vegetables are tender.
Stir in the chopped spinach or kale and let it wilt into the stew.
Add the soy sauce or tamari, brown sugar or maple syrup, and lime juice to the stew. Season with salt and pepper to taste.
Simmer the stew for another 5 minutes to allow the flavors to meld together.
Serve the Thai Curry Chickpea Stew hot, ladled over cooked rice or quinoa.

Garnish with chopped fresh cilantro before serving.

Enjoy this flavorful and nutritious Thai Curry Chickpea Stew as a satisfying meal on its own or as a comforting dish served with rice or quinoa!

Thai Curry Vegetable Spring Rolls

Ingredients:

- 8-10 spring roll wrappers (rice paper)
- 1 small cucumber, julienned
- 1 carrot, julienned
- 1 bell pepper (any color), thinly sliced
- 1/2 cup shredded purple cabbage
- 1/2 cup fresh cilantro leaves
- 1/2 cup fresh mint leaves
- 1/2 cup cooked rice vermicelli noodles
- Thai red curry paste, to taste
- Peanut sauce or sweet chili sauce, for dipping (optional)

Instructions:

Prepare all your vegetables and herbs by washing, peeling, and julienning them. Also, cook the rice vermicelli noodles according to package instructions, then rinse them with cold water and drain well.

Fill a shallow dish or pie plate with warm water. Dip one rice paper wrapper into the water for about 15-20 seconds until it softens. Be careful not to over-soak it, as it will become too fragile to work with.

Place the softened rice paper wrapper on a clean, damp kitchen towel or a smooth surface.

Layer a small amount of each prepared vegetable, herbs, and rice vermicelli noodles on the bottom third of the rice paper wrapper, leaving some space on the sides to fold.

Optionally, spread a small amount of Thai red curry paste over the vegetables for added flavor.

Fold the bottom of the rice paper wrapper over the filling, then fold in the sides, and roll tightly to enclose the filling completely.

Repeat the process with the remaining rice paper wrappers and filling ingredients.

Serve the Thai Curry Vegetable Spring Rolls immediately with peanut sauce or sweet chili sauce for dipping, if desired.

Enjoy these Thai Curry Vegetable Spring Rolls as a light and flavorful appetizer or snack! They're perfect for serving at parties, picnics, or as a refreshing summer treat.

Thai Curry Breakfast Hash

Ingredients:

- 2 tablespoons vegetable oil
- 1 onion, diced
- 2 cloves garlic, minced
- 1 tablespoon grated ginger
- 2 tablespoons Thai red curry paste
- 2 medium sweet potatoes, peeled and diced
- 1 red bell pepper, diced
- 1 yellow bell pepper, diced
- 1 cup diced cooked chicken or tofu (optional)
- 1 cup cooked quinoa or rice
- Salt and pepper, to taste
- Fresh cilantro, chopped, for garnish
- Fried or poached eggs, for serving (optional)

Instructions:

Heat the vegetable oil in a large skillet or frying pan over medium heat.
Add the diced onion to the skillet and cook until softened, about 3-4 minutes.
Stir in the minced garlic, grated ginger, and Thai red curry paste, and cook for another 1-2 minutes, until fragrant.
Add the diced sweet potatoes to the skillet and cook, stirring occasionally, for about 8-10 minutes, or until they are tender and lightly browned.
Add the diced bell peppers to the skillet and cook for an additional 3-4 minutes, until they are softened.
If using, add the diced cooked chicken or tofu to the skillet and cook until heated through, about 2-3 minutes.
Stir in the cooked quinoa or rice and mix well with the vegetables and protein.
Season the Thai Curry Breakfast Hash with salt and pepper to taste.
Garnish with chopped fresh cilantro before serving.
Serve the breakfast hash hot, optionally topped with fried or poached eggs for extra protein.

Enjoy this flavorful and satisfying Thai Curry Breakfast Hash as a delicious and hearty breakfast or brunch option!

Thai Curry Butternut Squash Soup

Ingredients:

- 1 medium butternut squash (about 2 lbs), peeled, seeded, and cubed
- 1 tablespoon olive oil
- 1 onion, chopped
- 3 cloves garlic, minced
- 1 tablespoon grated ginger
- 2 tablespoons Thai red curry paste
- 4 cups vegetable broth
- 1 can (14 oz) coconut milk
- 1 tablespoon soy sauce or tamari
- 1 tablespoon brown sugar or maple syrup
- Juice of 1 lime
- Salt and pepper, to taste
- Optional garnish: chopped fresh cilantro, sliced green onions, toasted pumpkin seeds

Instructions:

Preheat your oven to 400°F (200°C). Place the cubed butternut squash on a baking sheet lined with parchment paper. Drizzle with olive oil and toss to coat. Roast the butternut squash in the preheated oven for 25-30 minutes, or until tender and caramelized. Remove from the oven and set aside.
In a large pot or Dutch oven, heat a tablespoon of olive oil over medium heat. Add the chopped onion and cook until softened, about 5 minutes.
Add the minced garlic, grated ginger, and Thai red curry paste to the pot. Cook for another 1-2 minutes, stirring constantly, until fragrant.
Add the roasted butternut squash cubes to the pot, followed by the vegetable broth. Stir to combine.
Bring the mixture to a simmer and let it cook for about 10-15 minutes, allowing the flavors to meld together.
Use an immersion blender to puree the soup until smooth and creamy. Alternatively, you can carefully transfer the soup in batches to a blender and blend until smooth, then return it to the pot.
Stir in the coconut milk, soy sauce or tamari, brown sugar or maple syrup, and lime juice. Season with salt and pepper to taste.
Simmer the soup for another 5 minutes to heat through.

Ladle the Thai Curry Butternut Squash Soup into bowls and garnish with chopped fresh cilantro, sliced green onions, and toasted pumpkin seeds if desired. Serve hot and enjoy!

This Thai Curry Butternut Squash Soup is perfect for warming up on a chilly day and makes a satisfying meal on its own or paired with crusty bread or a salad.

Thai Curry Pita Pockets

Ingredients:

- 4 whole wheat pita bread rounds
- 1 cup cooked chicken, shredded (optional)
- 1 cup cooked quinoa or rice
- 1 cup mixed vegetables (such as bell peppers, carrots, cucumbers, and lettuce), thinly sliced or shredded
- 1/4 cup Thai red curry paste
- 1/4 cup coconut milk
- 1 tablespoon lime juice
- 1 tablespoon soy sauce or tamari
- 1 tablespoon brown sugar or maple syrup
- Salt and pepper, to taste
- Fresh cilantro leaves, chopped, for garnish (optional)

Instructions:

In a small bowl, whisk together the Thai red curry paste, coconut milk, lime juice, soy sauce or tamari, and brown sugar or maple syrup to make the sauce. Adjust the seasoning to taste with salt and pepper.
If using cooked chicken, shred it into bite-sized pieces.
Warm the pita bread rounds in a toaster or oven until slightly softened and warm.
Carefully cut open each pita bread round to form a pocket.
Stuff each pita pocket with cooked quinoa or rice, shredded chicken (if using), and mixed vegetables.
Drizzle the Thai curry sauce over the filling in each pita pocket.
Garnish with chopped fresh cilantro leaves, if desired.
Serve the Thai Curry Pita Pockets immediately, and enjoy!

These Thai Curry Pita Pockets make a delicious and convenient meal for lunch or dinner. They're also great for packing in lunches or picnics. Feel free to customize the filling with your favorite ingredients for a personalized touch!

Thai Curry Rice Paper Rolls

Ingredients:

- 8-10 rice paper wrappers
- 1 cup cooked vermicelli noodles, cooled
- 1 cup cooked chicken, shrimp, tofu, or tempeh (optional), sliced or shredded
- 1 cup mixed vegetables (such as shredded carrots, cucumber, bell pepper, lettuce, and avocado)
- Fresh herbs (such as cilantro, mint, and basil)
- Thai red curry paste
- 1/4 cup coconut milk
- 1 tablespoon soy sauce or tamari
- 1 tablespoon lime juice
- 1 teaspoon brown sugar or maple syrup
- Crushed peanuts or cashews, for garnish (optional)
- Sweet chili sauce or peanut sauce, for dipping

Instructions:

Prepare all your ingredients and set them out in an assembly line for easy rolling.
In a small bowl, whisk together the Thai red curry paste, coconut milk, soy sauce or tamari, lime juice, and brown sugar or maple syrup to make the dipping sauce. Adjust the seasoning to taste.
Fill a shallow dish with warm water. Dip one rice paper wrapper into the water for about 10-15 seconds until it softens. Be careful not to over-soak it, as it will become too fragile to work with.
Place the softened rice paper wrapper on a clean, damp kitchen towel or a smooth surface.
Layer a small amount of each filling ingredient (cooked vermicelli noodles, protein, mixed vegetables, and fresh herbs) on the bottom third of the rice paper wrapper, leaving some space on the sides to fold.
Drizzle a small amount of the Thai curry dipping sauce over the filling.
Fold the bottom of the rice paper wrapper over the filling, then fold in the sides, and roll tightly to enclose the filling completely.
Repeat the process with the remaining rice paper wrappers and filling ingredients.
Serve the Thai Curry Rice Paper Rolls immediately with crushed peanuts or cashews for garnish and sweet chili sauce or peanut sauce for dipping.

These Thai Curry Rice Paper Rolls are perfect for a light and refreshing appetizer, snack, or even a main dish. They're great for entertaining or for a healthy meal on-the-go!

Thai Curry Veggie Burgers

Ingredients:

For the Veggie Patties:

2 cups cooked chickpeas, drained and rinsed

1 cup cooked quinoa or brown rice

1 small onion, finely chopped

2 cloves garlic, minced

1 tablespoon Thai red curry paste

1 tablespoon soy sauce or tamari

1 tablespoon lime juice

1 tablespoon brown sugar or maple syrup

1 teaspoon ground cumin

1/2 teaspoon ground coriander

Salt and pepper, to taste

1/4 cup breadcrumbs or oat flour (optional, for binding)

2 tablespoons vegetable oil, for cooking

For Serving:

Burger buns or lettuce wraps

Sliced tomatoes

Sliced cucumber

Fresh lettuce or spinach leaves

Thai sweet chili sauce or peanut sauce

Fresh cilantro leaves, for garnish

Instructions:

In a food processor, combine the cooked chickpeas, cooked quinoa or brown rice, chopped onion, minced garlic, Thai red curry paste, soy sauce or tamari, lime juice, brown sugar or maple syrup, ground cumin, and ground coriander. Pulse until the mixture is well combined but still slightly chunky.

If the mixture is too wet, add breadcrumbs or oat flour, a little at a time, until it reaches a firm consistency that can be shaped into patties. If it's too dry, add a splash of water or vegetable broth.

Divide the mixture into equal portions and shape them into patties.

Heat vegetable oil in a large skillet over medium heat. Once hot, add the patties to the skillet and cook for 4-5 minutes on each side, or until golden brown and heated through.

While the patties are cooking, prepare your burger buns or lettuce wraps and slice the tomatoes and cucumber.

Assemble the Thai Curry Veggie Burgers by placing a patty on a bun or lettuce leaf, then layering with sliced tomatoes, cucumber, and lettuce or spinach leaves.

Drizzle Thai sweet chili sauce or peanut sauce over the toppings and garnish with fresh cilantro leaves.

Serve the burgers immediately and enjoy!

These Thai Curry Veggie Burgers are packed with flavor and nutrients, making them a delicious and satisfying option for lunch or dinner. Feel free to customize the toppings and sauces according to your preference!

Thai Curry Couscous Salad

Ingredients:

- 1 cup couscous
- 1 1/4 cups vegetable broth or water
- 1 tablespoon olive oil
- 1 tablespoon Thai red curry paste
- 1 tablespoon soy sauce or tamari
- 1 tablespoon lime juice
- 1 teaspoon brown sugar or maple syrup
- 1 red bell pepper, diced
- 1 cucumber, diced
- 1 carrot, grated
- 1/4 cup chopped fresh cilantro
- 1/4 cup chopped green onions
- 1/4 cup roasted peanuts or cashews, chopped (optional)
- Salt and pepper, to taste

Instructions:

In a medium saucepan, bring the vegetable broth or water to a boil. Once boiling, remove from heat and stir in the couscous. Cover and let it sit for 5 minutes, or until the couscous is fluffy and all the liquid is absorbed.

In a small bowl, whisk together the olive oil, Thai red curry paste, soy sauce or tamari, lime juice, and brown sugar or maple syrup to make the dressing.

Fluff the cooked couscous with a fork to separate the grains and transfer it to a large mixing bowl.

Pour the dressing over the couscous and toss to coat evenly.

Add the diced red bell pepper, diced cucumber, grated carrot, chopped cilantro, and chopped green onions to the bowl with the dressed couscous. Toss until well combined.

If using, sprinkle chopped roasted peanuts or cashews over the salad for added crunch and flavor.

Season the salad with salt and pepper to taste.

Serve the Thai Curry Couscous Salad chilled or at room temperature, and enjoy!

This Thai Curry Couscous Salad is perfect as a light and refreshing side dish or as a standalone meal. It's versatile and can be customized with additional vegetables or protein sources according to your preference.

Thai Curry Roasted Brussels Sprouts

Ingredients:

- 1 lb Brussels sprouts, trimmed and halved
- 2 tablespoons olive oil
- 2 tablespoons Thai red curry paste
- 1 tablespoon soy sauce or tamari
- 1 tablespoon maple syrup or honey
- 1 tablespoon lime juice
- 2 cloves garlic, minced
- 1 teaspoon grated fresh ginger
- Salt and pepper, to taste
- Optional garnish: chopped fresh cilantro, lime wedges

Instructions:

Preheat your oven to 400°F (200°C). Line a baking sheet with parchment paper or aluminum foil for easy cleanup.

In a large bowl, whisk together the olive oil, Thai red curry paste, soy sauce or tamari, maple syrup or honey, lime juice, minced garlic, and grated ginger until well combined.

Add the trimmed and halved Brussels sprouts to the bowl with the curry mixture. Toss until the Brussels sprouts are evenly coated.

Spread the coated Brussels sprouts in a single layer on the prepared baking sheet.

Season the Brussels sprouts with salt and pepper to taste.

Roast the Brussels sprouts in the preheated oven for 20-25 minutes, or until they are tender and caramelized, stirring halfway through the cooking time for even browning.

Once the Brussels sprouts are roasted to your liking, remove them from the oven and transfer them to a serving dish.

Garnish the Thai Curry Roasted Brussels Sprouts with chopped fresh cilantro and serve with lime wedges on the side for squeezing, if desired.

Serve hot as a delicious and flavorful side dish.

Enjoy these Thai Curry Roasted Brussels Sprouts as a flavorful and nutritious addition to your meal!

Thai Curry Zoodle Salad

Ingredients:

- 4 medium zucchini, spiralized into noodles
- 1 red bell pepper, thinly sliced
- 1 carrot, julienned
- 1/4 cup chopped fresh cilantro
- 1/4 cup chopped fresh mint leaves
- 1/4 cup chopped roasted peanuts or cashews
- Optional protein: cooked shrimp, chicken, tofu, or chickpeas

For the Thai Curry Dressing:

- 1/4 cup light coconut milk
- 2 tablespoons lime juice
- 2 tablespoons Thai red curry paste
- 1 tablespoon soy sauce or tamari
- 1 tablespoon honey or maple syrup
- 1 tablespoon olive oil
- 2 cloves garlic, minced
- 1 teaspoon grated fresh ginger
- Salt and pepper, to taste

Instructions:

In a small bowl, whisk together all the ingredients for the Thai Curry Dressing until well combined. Taste and adjust seasoning as needed.
In a large mixing bowl, combine the spiralized zucchini noodles, thinly sliced red bell pepper, julienned carrot, chopped fresh cilantro, and chopped fresh mint leaves.
If adding protein, toss it with the salad ingredients.
Pour the Thai Curry Dressing over the salad and toss until everything is well coated.
Sprinkle chopped roasted peanuts or cashews over the salad just before serving.
Serve the Thai Curry Zoodle Salad immediately, and enjoy!

This Thai Curry Zoodle Salad is light, refreshing, and bursting with Thai flavors. It makes a perfect lunch or dinner option, and you can easily customize it with your favorite protein or additional vegetables.

Thai Curry Corn Chowder

Ingredients:

- 4 cups fresh or frozen corn kernels
- 1 tablespoon vegetable oil
- 1 onion, chopped
- 2 cloves garlic, minced
- 1 tablespoon Thai red curry paste
- 1 can (14 oz) coconut milk
- 4 cups vegetable broth
- 2 medium potatoes, peeled and diced
- 1 red bell pepper, diced
- 1 carrot, diced
- 1 teaspoon grated fresh ginger
- 1 teaspoon ground turmeric
- 1 tablespoon soy sauce or tamari
- 1 tablespoon lime juice
- Salt and pepper, to taste
- Fresh cilantro leaves, chopped, for garnish
- Lime wedges, for serving (optional)

Instructions:

In a large pot or Dutch oven, heat the vegetable oil over medium heat. Add the chopped onion and cook until softened, about 5 minutes.

Add the minced garlic and Thai red curry paste to the pot. Cook for another 1-2 minutes, stirring constantly, until fragrant.

Pour in the coconut milk and vegetable broth, stirring to combine.

Add the diced potatoes, diced red bell pepper, diced carrot, grated ginger, and ground turmeric to the pot. Stir to combine.

Bring the mixture to a simmer and let it cook for about 15-20 minutes, or until the potatoes are tender.

Add the corn kernels to the pot and cook for an additional 5 minutes.

Stir in the soy sauce or tamari and lime juice. Season with salt and pepper to taste.

Use an immersion blender to partially blend the soup until creamy but still chunky. Alternatively, you can carefully transfer a portion of the soup to a blender and blend until smooth, then return it to the pot.

Serve the Thai Curry Corn Chowder hot, garnished with chopped fresh cilantro and lime wedges on the side for squeezing, if desired.

This Thai Curry Corn Chowder is creamy, flavorful, and comforting, making it perfect for a cozy meal on a chilly day. Enjoy its unique fusion of Thai and comfort food flavors!

Thai Curry Pizza

Ingredients:

For the pizza dough:

- 1 package (0.25 oz) active dry yeast
- 1 cup warm water
- 1 teaspoon sugar
- 2 1/2 cups all-purpose flour
- 1 tablespoon olive oil
- 1 teaspoon salt

For the Thai Curry Sauce:

- 1/4 cup Thai red curry paste
- 1 can (14 oz) coconut milk
- 2 tablespoons soy sauce or tamari
- 1 tablespoon lime juice
- 1 tablespoon brown sugar or maple syrup
- 2 cloves garlic, minced
- 1 teaspoon grated fresh ginger
- Salt and pepper, to taste

For the toppings:

- 1 cup cooked and shredded chicken, tofu, or shrimp
- 1 red bell pepper, thinly sliced
- 1/2 red onion, thinly sliced
- 1/2 cup shredded mozzarella cheese
- 1/4 cup chopped fresh cilantro
- 1/4 cup chopped roasted peanuts or cashews

Instructions:

1. Prepare the pizza dough:

    In a small bowl, combine the warm water, sugar, and active dry yeast. Let it sit for about 5-10 minutes, or until foamy.
    In a large mixing bowl, combine the flour and salt. Gradually add the yeast mixture and olive oil, stirring until a dough forms.

Turn the dough out onto a lightly floured surface and knead for about 5 minutes, or until smooth and elastic. Place the dough in a greased bowl, cover with a clean kitchen towel, and let it rise in a warm place for about 1 hour, or until doubled in size.

2. Prepare the Thai Curry Sauce:

In a saucepan, combine the Thai red curry paste, coconut milk, soy sauce or tamari, lime juice, brown sugar or maple syrup, minced garlic, and grated ginger. Bring the mixture to a simmer over medium heat.
Cook, stirring occasionally, for about 5-7 minutes, or until the sauce has thickened slightly. Season with salt and pepper to taste. Remove from heat and set aside.

3. Assemble and bake the pizza:

Preheat your oven to 475°F (245°C). If you have a pizza stone, place it in the oven to preheat as well.
Punch down the risen pizza dough and divide it into two equal portions. Roll out each portion into a round shape on a lightly floured surface.
Transfer the rolled-out dough onto a parchment paper-lined baking sheet or a pizza peel if using a pizza stone.
Spread a generous amount of the prepared Thai Curry Sauce over each pizza dough, leaving a small border around the edges.
Top the pizzas with shredded chicken, tofu, or shrimp, sliced red bell pepper, and sliced red onion. Sprinkle shredded mozzarella cheese over the toppings.
Transfer the pizzas to the preheated oven and bake for 12-15 minutes, or until the crust is golden brown and the cheese is melted and bubbly.
Remove the pizzas from the oven and sprinkle chopped fresh cilantro and chopped roasted peanuts or cashews over the top.
Slice the Thai Curry Pizza into wedges and serve hot.

Enjoy this unique and flavorful Thai Curry Pizza as a delicious twist on the classic favorite!

Thai Curry Chickpea Curry

Ingredients:

- 2 tablespoons vegetable oil
- 1 onion, finely chopped
- 3 cloves garlic, minced
- 1 tablespoon grated ginger
- 2 tablespoons Thai red curry paste
- 1 can (14 oz) coconut milk
- 2 cans (15 oz each) chickpeas, drained and rinsed
- 1 red bell pepper, diced
- 1 zucchini, diced
- 1 cup diced tomatoes (fresh or canned)
- 1 cup vegetable broth
- 1 tablespoon soy sauce or tamari
- 1 tablespoon brown sugar or maple syrup
- Juice of 1 lime
- Salt and pepper, to taste
- Fresh cilantro leaves, chopped, for garnish
- Cooked rice or naan bread, for serving

Instructions:

In a large pot or skillet, heat the vegetable oil over medium heat. Add the chopped onion and cook until softened, about 5 minutes.
Add the minced garlic and grated ginger to the pot and cook for an additional 1-2 minutes, until fragrant.
Stir in the Thai red curry paste and cook for another minute to toast the spices.
Pour in the coconut milk and vegetable broth, stirring to combine.
Add the drained and rinsed chickpeas, diced red bell pepper, diced zucchini, and diced tomatoes to the pot. Stir to combine.
Bring the mixture to a simmer and let it cook for about 15-20 minutes, until the vegetables are tender and the flavors have melded together.
Stir in the soy sauce or tamari, brown sugar or maple syrup, and lime juice.
Season with salt and pepper to taste.
Simmer the chickpea curry for another 5 minutes to allow the flavors to develop.
Serve the Thai Curry Chickpea Curry hot, ladled over cooked rice or accompanied by naan bread.
Garnish with chopped fresh cilantro before serving.

Enjoy this delicious and aromatic Thai Curry Chickpea Curry as a satisfying and comforting meal!

Thai Curry Cucumber Salad

Ingredients:

- 2 cucumbers, thinly sliced
- 1/4 cup chopped red onion
- 1/4 cup chopped fresh cilantro
- 1/4 cup chopped roasted peanuts or cashews
- Optional: 1 small red chili, thinly sliced (for added heat)

For the Dressing:

- 2 tablespoons rice vinegar
- 1 tablespoon soy sauce or tamari
- 1 tablespoon Thai red curry paste
- 1 tablespoon honey or maple syrup
- 1 tablespoon lime juice
- 1 clove garlic, minced
- 1 teaspoon grated fresh ginger
- Salt and pepper, to taste

Instructions:

In a small bowl, whisk together all the ingredients for the dressing until well combined. Taste and adjust seasoning as needed.

In a large mixing bowl, combine the thinly sliced cucumbers, chopped red onion, chopped cilantro, and chopped roasted peanuts or cashews. If using, add the thinly sliced red chili for added heat.

Pour the dressing over the cucumber mixture and toss until everything is well coated.

Let the salad marinate in the refrigerator for at least 30 minutes before serving to allow the flavors to meld together.

Serve the Thai Curry Cucumber Salad chilled as a refreshing side dish alongside your favorite Thai-inspired main course.

Enjoy this vibrant and flavorful Thai Curry Cucumber Salad as a light and refreshing addition to your meal!

Thai Curry Quinoa Salad

Ingredients:

- 1 cup quinoa, rinsed
- 2 cups water or vegetable broth
- 1 red bell pepper, diced
- 1 yellow bell pepper, diced
- 1 cucumber, diced
- 1/2 cup shredded carrots
- 1/4 cup chopped fresh cilantro
- 1/4 cup chopped fresh mint leaves
- 1/4 cup chopped roasted peanuts or cashews
- Optional: 1 small red chili, thinly sliced (for added heat)

For the Dressing:

- 1/4 cup light coconut milk
- 2 tablespoons Thai red curry paste
- 2 tablespoons lime juice
- 1 tablespoon soy sauce or tamari
- 1 tablespoon honey or maple syrup
- 1 clove garlic, minced
- 1 teaspoon grated fresh ginger
- Salt and pepper, to taste

Instructions:

In a medium saucepan, combine the rinsed quinoa and water or vegetable broth. Bring to a boil over medium-high heat.
Reduce the heat to low, cover, and simmer for 15-20 minutes, or until the quinoa is cooked and the liquid is absorbed. Remove from heat and let it cool.
In a large mixing bowl, combine the cooked and cooled quinoa, diced red bell pepper, diced yellow bell pepper, diced cucumber, shredded carrots, chopped cilantro, chopped mint leaves, and chopped roasted peanuts or cashews. If using, add the thinly sliced red chili for added heat.
In a small bowl, whisk together all the ingredients for the dressing until well combined. Taste and adjust seasoning as needed.
Pour the dressing over the quinoa salad and toss until everything is well coated.

Serve the Thai Curry Quinoa Salad chilled or at room temperature as a delicious and nutritious side dish or main course.

Enjoy this flavorful and vibrant Thai Curry Quinoa Salad as a satisfying meal or accompaniment to your favorite Thai-inspired dishes!

Thai Curry Ratatouille

Ingredients:

- 1 eggplant, diced
- 2 zucchinis, diced
- 2 bell peppers (any color), diced
- 1 onion, diced
- 2 tomatoes, diced
- 3 cloves garlic, minced
- 2 tablespoons Thai red curry paste
- 1 can (14 oz) coconut milk
- 2 tablespoons vegetable oil
- Salt and pepper to taste
- Fresh basil leaves, chopped, for garnish

Instructions:

Heat the vegetable oil in a large skillet or Dutch oven over medium heat.
Add the diced onion and minced garlic to the skillet and cook until softened, about 5 minutes.
Stir in the Thai red curry paste and cook for another minute to release the flavors.
Add the diced eggplant, zucchini, bell peppers, and tomatoes to the skillet. Stir well to coat the vegetables with the curry paste mixture.
Pour in the coconut milk and stir to combine.
Season with salt and pepper to taste.
Cover the skillet and let the mixture simmer over medium-low heat for about 20-25 minutes, or until the vegetables are tender.
Once the vegetables are cooked through, remove the skillet from heat.
Garnish with chopped fresh basil leaves before serving.
Serve the Thai Curry Ratatouille hot, accompanied by rice or crusty bread.

Enjoy this flavorful and aromatic Thai Curry Ratatouille as a comforting and satisfying meal!

Thai Curry Potato Salad

Ingredients:

- 2 lbs potatoes (such as Yukon Gold or red potatoes), peeled and cubed
- 1/4 cup mayonnaise
- 1/4 cup Greek yogurt or sour cream
- 2 tablespoons Thai red curry paste
- 2 tablespoons lime juice
- 1 tablespoon honey or maple syrup
- 1 teaspoon grated fresh ginger
- 1 clove garlic, minced
- Salt and pepper, to taste
- 1/4 cup chopped fresh cilantro
- Optional: 1/4 cup chopped green onions or red onions for garnish
- Optional: Crushed roasted peanuts or cashews for garnish

Instructions:

Place the cubed potatoes in a large pot and cover with water. Add a pinch of salt to the water. Bring to a boil over medium-high heat, then reduce the heat to medium-low and simmer for 10-15 minutes, or until the potatoes are fork-tender. While the potatoes are cooking, prepare the dressing. In a small bowl, whisk together the mayonnaise, Greek yogurt or sour cream, Thai red curry paste, lime juice, honey or maple syrup, grated ginger, minced garlic, salt, and pepper until smooth and well combined.
Once the potatoes are cooked, drain them and transfer them to a large mixing bowl. Let them cool slightly.
Pour the prepared dressing over the warm potatoes and toss gently to coat evenly.
Add the chopped fresh cilantro to the potato salad and toss again to distribute. Taste and adjust seasoning as needed, adding more salt, pepper, or lime juice if desired.
Garnish the Thai Curry Potato Salad with chopped green onions or red onions and crushed roasted peanuts or cashews, if using.
Serve the potato salad immediately, or cover and refrigerate for at least an hour to allow the flavors to meld together before serving.

Enjoy this flavorful and creamy Thai Curry Potato Salad as a delicious side dish for picnics, barbecues, or any meal!

www.ingramcontent.com/pod-product-compliance
Lightning Source LLC
LaVergne TN
LVHW062051070526
838201LV00080B/2309